THE ORDER OF THE DAY

Also by Andrew Greig

POETRY
White Boats (Garret Arts, 1972)
Men On Ice (Canongate, 1977)
Surviving Passages (Canongate, 1982)
A Flame in Your Heart, with Kathleen Jamie
    (Bloodaxe Books, 1986)

MOUNTAINEERING
Summit Fever (Hutchinson, 1985)
Kingdoms of Experience (Hutchinson, 1986)

)

THE ORDER OF THE DAY

Andrew Greig

BLOODAXE BOOKS

ISBN: 1 85224 102 0

First published 1990 by
Bloodaxe Books Ltd,
P.O. Box 1SN,
Newcastle upon Tyne NE99 1SN.

Bloodaxe Books Ltd acknowledges
the financial assistance of Northern Arts

Typesetting by Bryan Williamson, Darwen, Lancashire.

Printed in Great Britain by
Billings & Sons Limited, Worcester.

For my father, who over his lifetime went
from Red Clydeside to Old Tory but aye said
'No one ever got rich but at the expense of
the widow, the orphan, or the stranger at the door'.

And my mother, who sang when I was wee

> 'Far across the firmament
> The floating sausage blows
> He seeks his little frying pan,
> The only home he knows...'

Somewhere between them, this book.

To my friends -- thanks a bundle.

Acknowledgements

Acknowledgements are due to the editors of the following publications in which some of these poems first appeared: *Alpine Journal, Chapman, Gown, Landfall* (New Zealand), *Mountain, New Statesman, New Writing Scotland, Poetry Review, Poetry with an Edge* (Bloodaxe Books, 1988), *The Scotsman* and *Verse*. 'The Maid & I' was broadcast on *Poetry Now* (BBC Radio 3).

The author gratefully acknowledges the help of a Scottish Arts Council Writers' Bursary in completing this book.

The Order of the Day

IN THE MOUNTAINS

Back Again
On Lhotse Shar

We're back again
with our tents, our trash,
our high ambition. We've come
to be both audience and show.

Mal flicked his lighter,
an avalanche roared –
we have come to assert
everything fits

and we believe
the true scale of things
is the entire mountain
hung mirrored in our shades.

*

All day snow sank in the billy,
was boiled, drunk, peed, replenished
as we passed the mountain through us.
The chat was home and axes, hopes, seracs.

The voices tire, yellow lights
hiss as night comes on
to very few witnesses
but enough.

Unblinking stars and lightning –
the theatre's hushed.
From the heights we propose
to the depths we've left

our shadows gesture and stretch.

Interlude on Mustagh Tower

In these high places we are melting out
of all that made us rigid; our ice-screws
hang loose on the fixed ropes to the Col.
Monday in the Himalaya, the clouds are down,
our objective is somewhere, but obscure –
let it soar without us for a day!
We lounge in thermals on the glacier,
brewing and shooting the breeze, that improbable
project of conversation among the living.
Laughter rings across the ice. Why not?
None of us will die today – yon's immortality
you can draw on in a cigarette,
harsh and sweet, the way we like it.
Steam rises from the billy, Sandy pours.
It is true high, worked for, that we pass
hand to hand between us with our brews.
Men on ice, going nowhere and laughing
at everything we cannot see but know
is there – among the cloud, on the Col,
a hand of some sort is tightening our screws.

Sandy, Topping Out on Mustagh

So began to lead the last of the Tower
Quite hard   more bold than difficult
tough ice   loose snow   but soon brain
began to play the game   My points investigated
stabbed   good placements to be had
among loose choss   Crucified by altitude
I bridged a steepish rockwall   Good
value that   I remember everything
like ice-slivers in my windsuit's creases   Camp 4
a thousand feet beneath my heels   climbing
into my shadow   the sun
flashed off my axe
                    Jon he was somewhere
giving good rope and no advice   the ideal second
but me   I was gone

       Nice work when you can get it
       the hardest   the best   hours passed
       till I wanted a think and a rest
       so thumped in an ice-screw and hung out awhile –

              Like I cannot spell, speak porter-talk
              but who does not who's lived like me
              with oil roughnecks and a French girl?
              One look in her eyes, I know.
              One straight hit, I find good ice.
              Climbing's not so much, my life's more in
              the way I eat my food, the man I rise above,
              the roads I drive to friends,
              these suit –

       Re-engaged myself and winkled on
       with patient pickers unlocked the crux
       set my axes well and at full stretch
       pulled over the top and saw into China

felt ok   felt well
(à cheval across the summit)
K2 in the distance looking good
(suspicion of moisture behind my shades)

Made a belay and took in the ropes
as Jon came up. So how's it going?
Oh, wasted, youth...

*'From Base Camp to the stream there is a path now
and the grass is yellow at the centre of the path.'*

Entering Askole
(for Malcolm Duff)

On the eighth evening we entered Askole.
How can I tell you? We had seen
no habitation in two months. Brown dogs
twitched in the shade, a chicken screamed;
we smelled dung, dall, smoke, lentils;
many voices, the bronze fields shone.
Lean as schoolmasters, tall wheat rapped
our knuckles as we limped into the square.

Say there are miracles between
where babies twitch and sleep and old folk
sleep and totter. Water-mills spun,
yaks plonked circles round the threshing floor.
Evening prayers, a sleeping miller, tawny goats
stole husks of wheat. Goitres hung
like apples on the children's necks.
The Hadji lightly touched our backs, *Summit good...*

We had been above ourselves, hooked to
pure worlds of black & white & blue,
the narrow world of sleeping bags.
In Askole we smoked and talked till dawn
then rose and crossed the river,
paid the porters, jeep did the rest.
We broke down, sang 'It will come hard
to sleep on beds as soft and wide as ours.'

The Winter Climbing
(for Marj)

It is late January and at last the snow.
I lie back dreaming about Glencoe
as fluent, hungry, dressed in red,
you climb up and over me. That passion
claimed the darkest, useless months
for risk and play. You rise
up on me, I rise through you...

The shadowed face of Aonach Dubh
where Mal first took me climbing
and as we clanked exhausted, happy,
downwards through the dark, I asked
'What route was that?' 'Call it
what you want – it's new.'

You reach the top and exit out;
from way above, your cry comes down.
The rope pulls tight. What shall we call
this new thing we're about?
These days we live in taking
care and chances. Why name it?
My heart is in my mouth as I shout *Climbing*...

Crux

Delicate, hell-cat, at the crux on Hoy,
last word in day-long converse
with rock above deep blue, climbing
into pale blue, aiming for grace –
A hard way to be normal. The gods of agility
took him this far, 800 feet, soloing
and high on that mug's game.
Now they desert him. His fingers stutter
below the bulge – he's run out of ways
to speak to sandstone. Gripped? Mummified.
This rock is smooth as political tongues.

Hung from a hand-jam,
rock crystals enquire of his skin
How much you want to live, sweet youth?
Some questions draw blood and pride
equally, he answers, smears his right foot,
gets his left edged high. Chalk-bag,
pinch-grip...Now he's kiltered out,
all trussed up and nowhere to go.
The world waits with casual interest.
Gooseflesh, a draught blows through
from the next world – *going there soon?*

Adhesion's mostly faith for intricate movers
but he's shivering agnostic now
releasing the hand-jam he
s t r e t c h e s
                    his right boot slips
right hand up
                    fast as a prayer
grabs his Grail o lovely jug
then cranks like a maniac over the bulge.
Thugged it to the top, sat and was blank,
was gone, was everywhere in Orkney longlight...

We met him in Stromness, it was etched
in his eyes he'd dipped deep into more
than his chalk-bag that day.
White as cocaine his fingers
drummed the bar, awaiting tequila.
'Been pushing the envelope, matey?'
His eyes were mica as he considered
our question, glinting and flakey his smile:
'Aye, licked the stamp too.' Revving kite
on a taut string, could plummet or soar –
delicate hell-cat, you'll do.

Three Above Namche Bazaar
Heading for Lhotse

Sandy, feeling somewhat queasy,
squatted above Namche,
shat a foot-long worm. My life's
like that, he said as we
laughed and took our photographs,
a thread of consistency
through unconsolidated crap.
                – All things pass
as expeditions through the Bazaar,
joking & jiving & ripping each other off.
Got a bad feeling about this trip, boss.

Some days you scoff and scoff
but just get thinner,
Mal grinned. Had a friend,
dead now, he always swallowed
a tape-worm before he came this way –
never got ill. He'd say
just to be here, we must have been promoted.
                – Think that's true?
A monk once stopped me on the trail
below Temboche monastery, said he
saw death in my eyes, now I'm wondering whose.

We rounded the corner and there –
the big Mothers: Nuptse, Lhotse, Everest.
My heart battered
                in my chest
like a man
              beating
on the walls   of the cage
           surrounding him

     and I thought
             huh   Climbing –

this bad bug kills off all the rest.

After Everest

Between one expedition and the next
we buried the tiny Buddha's bones
upright, with respect,
at the bottom of the garden.

Then we were driven
back to the mountain.

Between the highway and the ditch
the restless West
verges on its limit...

No one said we are too old
to die young, too young to retire
as we left Lhasa in dust.

Avalanche

He's at it again,
first time in years
a woman's hips hands eyes,
wherever the categorical resides,
have issued the imperative
Screw our lights out.
Hot bulb! (Cooling in the dark.)

He dreams of avalanche
quick & white & casual...

Waking in sheets
he regards her where she lies face down.
The terror lies
in the tenderness derived
between the slope and shiftings of her ribs.

IN LOVE & POLITICS

A Reader's Note

Call him anything, call him Jim. At any road
a Scottish male of a certain age
stands hopeful, hesitating, lost.
He scuffs the dust, unable to go on or back.

I want to see him on the rack.
Compressed or stretched, the heresies will show.
And mock him carefully, you who go
to govern or deplore, judging
or not judging, in all events undone.

The riders of our times left notes behind
of intrigues high and low; one sings of love,
another of the shredding of a document...

He scans these tales of power – screwed up,
corrupt, infolded, though I would not have it so.

Mazed

It was the things the women *said*
fair mazed our Jim; contrary shocks
crazed him as they do with rats.
First they taught him *sensitivity*, to chop
onions very fine and cry, *prioritise*
the lady of his life. He got the knack.
Applause! Then she whose absence still defines

these screwey situations, left to flame it
with his pal Bill. *Live for friends, get in touch
with your distress.* But soon enough
his distresses got in touch with him –
a right good kicking filled him in.
His bruises were stupendous; in diverse beds
he was rewarded, sundry titbits showered on him.

Then Jenny came from Aberdeen to say
*Enough. Binge-time is over, the cheese is moved.
Work, discipline, avoiding dread diseases
will be the key-notes of the 90s.
Without political understanding
there is only pain – go sniff it out.*

Certitude of the educators, high ground
of the women, tests of the high heid yins!
Quivering, ardent – a rapier, a whippet,
as easily broken – she raps him on the chest:
Now you must forget your feelings.

Sod this for a game of mazes. He resigns.
On his back for days, pinky feet in the air.
What you doing, Jim? Minding the ceiling, and its bars...

Shetland

He sailed for Shetland, very near the edge,
to bog & cliff & a celibate friend.
She did her helpless best by him.
He climbed all day and failed to fall.

Light-hoarding stars above her bed,
a full moon on the wall – he wanted to be dead,
and badly. *A mortal sin*, she said, *I tried it*.
Well, she was Catholic but that stuck.

No way out but up. At the crux
he clutched into the chimney's heart and heaved...

He taped his knuckles, she poured the wine.
Only reflected light this tenderness, but still
that night they lay like pardoned thieves – baffled, eased,
beside her moon, beneath her paper stars.

About Tess

She cocks her head, considers
another country, you. Smoke infiltrates your throat.
The rasp that says you're not dead yet
is the trigger of seductions.
'And do you ever,' she enquires,
'act on your irresolution?'

The bar's de-stabilised,
you colonise each other as
folkies sing of Nicaragua.

'All right,' one hand on hers, the other
grips your car keys, 'Why not?'
There are reasons, but they melt like wax.

Relax. Tonight you cross the border.
You cast huge shadows as you get into the car.

Tess, in Tunisia

Released,
she tilts over on her side.

'The Fall is only that,' she says
shaking sand from her hair,
'when your wish returns
to Paradise. Go on, forget her.'

She says we are inventing
new ways of shipping men and women
and all her art is aiming for
a raft that swimmers reach and share.

She says this that it may be so.

You did not worry as you lay
beached together through a starless night;
an obscured moon still pulls the tides
of billow-talk and pillow-friends.

These words come
from Proverbs, Tess, and the Koran;
dogs bark above our heads and yet
the caravan moves on.

Love-Torn Squaddie in Rannoch Torment

Being, show me your ground.

Only the moor and a keep
of castellated cloud and the wind
moving on as she did, snagged
enough to make roots whine
like children left behind.

He waits for his heart to stop but it won't.

That's all the ground there is, soldier,
it's all ground, even the airy-fairy
cloud-castle on the hill, even
the shrilling in your chest.

Being torn between moving on
and being left behind, he wavers
shredded among heather.

Still

Here is stillness, there is still more
while the light is fading. Hands slow
then settle, they could meditate
or just be resting while birds pour
late songs from TV aerials.
Now whatever is trying to find you,
finds you; tea-pot, vase, radio
begin to shine, the early stars tune in.

Where are you when the light is fading?
Pulling on the red nightdress,
half-listening to the radio?
You are somewhere doing
something shadowy to me –
thanks be for that obscurity.
I loved you once; now you've gone dim
I still love someone, that is bearable.

This is the dusk of loving;
the birds are empty and these
are little sorrows, pin-prick ones.
Bearable instances, sad pretty stars
now dribble out above the last
note of the concluding song.
Here comes the calm, the insurmountable
parting. The aerial shakes still.

Annie, Visiting

'I went into your house
while you were away, I thought
so this is his chair, this is his cat,
here are the trainers he wears.

I sat in the chair and stroked the cat.
I sat on the cat and inspected the shoes:
a re-tied lace?
We've all tried that. It fails.
The heart, like your cat, sure is tough
but wails when sat on or scared –

This foolishness won't recur.
When you get home, I'll have gone running
miles from here. Catch as catch can,
if you're fit, if I tire, if we dare.'

Annie, in Spring

Life a dream? They're misinformed
who never laid a finger on your skin.

When you wake in spring
the fuzz on the pussy willow
and the willow itself are one:
nothing out of focus here.

The sun on our shoulders blooms, passes,
what more should we ask of light?
What is seen, is.
The eyes have it.

Now the sheen on the chestnut
and the chestnut itself
embrace in her hair,
there is no further waking.

Treaty

I love you, she says without triumph or apology,
then seeing his expression, adds
*Don't worry. I love also him and him
and her, my parents too.* That word so weighty,
who'd deploy it? He's puzzled but
something gives across his shoulders.

America and Russia made advances
meant to be rejected, broad & narrow
interpretations of a treaty. Now they're talking
verification, alliances. How did this happen?
They look at each other, puzzled but
something relaxes across the globe.

Reading Sunday papers it is clear
we could destroy each other. Yet may not.
From time to time, something lets up.
We are what we're devoted to, she said in spring
as outside birds proclaimed the laws
of mating and territory in our time.

Annie

In the Morning

The white cat at the window knows
being composed around itself.

Two mechanics lean over my car;
today's composed around what goes
and what does not – *New points, son,
condenser's gone.* The philosophical one
borrows a smoke, pokes the engine,
speaks of *Maya, the Veil of Illusion.*

Stuff and nonsense! This no-start's
stuff enough – *No problem, a tenner –*
that's the nonsense. Make it five?
Money's real too, there should be
more poems about money. *Six and it's done.*

This is not counterfeit. You're on.

In the Afternoon

So get cracking, hand me back
my life-enhancing cigarette!

That Veil: rend it as you will,
nothing's hung behind. Is she not
beautiful, tranced in the doorway?
In her breathed warm breath
there is no other.

Of course I'm scared – to love
and risk it while today
goes up in smoke! Go, roll
one of your own. My car goes,
our hearts ease off the brakes –

We're on a spin somewhere
the white cat at the window knows.

32

Gulf

Nothing is missing, said she
on Cairn Gorm, *world turns and we
turn with it, not losing touch.
I'll always love you   and   but*

In the Gulf
a frigate lowered its defensive screen
for a chat – men were blown away.

Sorry pal, I didn't mean…
The plane flew back to base
in some confusion.
Soon she did too.

Men yearn, metal yawns, verses implode
memory and daily news. Between I & I
the holy wars elide; between us rose
words – lovely, direct, misguided,
like love, an Exocet.

Annie, in November
A last pibroch in South Queensferry

Enough fourteen-bar compressed & gurgling
pibrochs for you, Annie, whoever you were
(I mythed you). There are affairs
more pressing than love, say they who have it.

So look around. The satellite disc
shines on the new deli; library hours are cut;
my neighbour's roof leaks into mine
(would we were separate, or one)...

The Chancellor parks his belly on TV,
proclaims Auld Scotia is a bag of wind
squeezed in History's oxter. Behind my town
the fields are burning, it is time to leave.

Rush hour. The trucks point North and whine
the wild notes, the low sun splits
the Road Bridge like a reed.

Ruth Says

This is not passion, but with pleasure
I see you note how well I am
undressed in black. Clear sight shows
our age, lines curved around the mouth
like brackets, as though we smile
as an aside (as though desire were
a little joke we like to tell
from time to time).

We are not in love, we are not drowning
in needy dreams, so we may lay down
our weary arms, unconfused
by fate and feeling; I am composed
as we surrender, eyes wide open
even as they close.

Spello, in the Afternoon

She has gone a long walk in the afternoon.
Only she knows
how close to home she is.

Her shadow on the road
shakes nothing where it passes –

the outline of a dress,
a coolness on the eyes,
it is scarcely more
than a manner of speaking.

Registered within
the steady lengthening
of all her gestures –

the by-blow of body and light,
coming home to one in the afternoon.

Nut

Love hammers on the roof with a starting handle,
yells 'Open up
so I can kill ya.' You must be joking.

It's been hard work, growing up.
He wants to stay an uncracked nut.
He lies in the bowl of the city
with a million others
going fousty at the heart.

None must pick him, he'll not nourish
causes, nor desire dangerous as guns...

But a hand is reaching down
and sorting through the streets towards him
comes one whose fingers could caress
or crack him like a flea.

Covert Action

Beneath the coverlet the President's mind
is acting up; he dreams
he is *the President*, which means
he is responsible. For what? The lot
of *The Free World* & dirty doings without number
such as haunted the Macbeths. Pick one:

Jungle, clearing, hut. Door's kicked down,
bullets fan the air; the wife, the son,
the daughter, redden and fold. Rocks
drop from their hands. Yup, guerillas!
The Peace Force torch the lot, exit right
up the sleeve of the star-spangled night...

To pay for this he must raise taxes!
He sweats, fumbles for light. Dreamed I wus
the President, he tells his wife.
You are, dear, you are. She sleeps
and sees the Nobel Prize for Peace
crowning hubby's noble head.

His pyjamas cling, the nightlight flickers,
Old Glory stirs upon the wall. Aw, who among us
lacks his Banquo? Pay the First Murderer,
let the drunken Security weep, for all the screw-ups
check in here. Who screams? Who knocks?
Mr President – it would make one mad, if not already so.

Young American

I sleep, I don't, she listed
all the heart-crimes I've committed.
Cover-ups, plots, double-cross, betrayal
in diverse jungles – truths most economical
swooped from her throat. Worse,

wheeling in her nightdress
she released her lovers' names.
Her words cling, burn
like our modern Nessus shirt, napalm. Worst,

when I wake there is no angry
young American at my side. Men cry
but are not cooled, just terrified;
the imperial wings
still burst above my head, within.

Fishing

He may love her when
he does not say 'I love you' then
hang on her reply. Who
does not go fishing
with such lines? Across the livingroom
her wrist flicks, the hook digs in.

In the kitchen he
is floundering – who knows when
to cut the line? He twists the tap
and sees down to the bottom.

He could leave coffee where she sits,
smile, say nothing, drift
into the garden...

She crochets steadily, taking him in.

D, in a Checked Shirt

I've chopped all day
and stacked my pile. Father taught me
no one else was good enough –
little wonder I
must work till I bleed, bop

till I drop at local dances.
I can split a match with a woodsman's axe
and have no lasting lovers.
The way I roll my sleeves, that final tuck's
my father; the shirt is yours

as I am mine – I've taken every risk
but that. Father told me:
give up nothing. So I don't
when I undress; you saw my eyes
when you asked me to unbutton more.

No can do. Your shirt is wringing
but I like sweating me
as you did. My body's perfect,
my skin tight as a drum,
nothing rattles me –

The perfect barbarian with a PhD
aches and lies down again, alone.
How that single candle spits and yearns!
Why should you call? The axe is bedded
in the log. I have a winter's burning.

D, Riding

Has found nothing could unhorse her yet
and so rides on, head up, heels down, believing
nothing ever will; fear's not admitted
to blue eyes shaded by a cowboy hat.
No grief's so ornery, she swears,
it can't be bridled, mounted, ridden

to some useful task. Listen,
those hands break horses to her will,
then with her sister on the grey
she rides down to the creek where men
hand-roll her cigarettes. Mother's blown
like tumbleweed, but she'll not be.

Once a month she may slump
saddle-weary on the endless plains
of an undulating blues harmonica,
when friends won't write or when a lover
moves on with his useful pair of hands.
But too much needs fixing round these parts

for private groaning, too many stray head
and idle hands for her to pine –
she straightens, flicks the reins again.
Something else, these assured young women
who have not lost, who train their luck
and ride it, sure they always will –

Get off with it? One day she'll be thrown
and twitching in the dirt will suss
she can't get up again. No blame,
but she'll be frightened and ashamed.
May someone be bending over her then,
hold out a hand and drawl 'Welcome

to the world of mortals, angel, it's tough
not being tough enough. Now impress me –
take my hand and with your other
salute those griefs we cannot master,
stumbling home behind them
as they stamp so proud.'

Heart & Irish

Your man's been ambushed by a holiday near Cork
years back with lady, Paud & Anne
with ½ acre marijuana and desire for children.
Peace broke out for days on end, fat pork
and laughter, winning at the dartboard & love...

With such memory, bent on re-uniting
or at least revenge (the unequal parting),
no peace for heart & Irish, no finis
to the troubles. On TV the funeral

wants blood, and his Mum says 'There's always
one who kisses, one who's kissed.' Who wins
the struggle? Whoever dares
to need it less. Anyway, the vehicle's doomed
when a man squats on the roof and lets rip.

Up the Baobab

Fiends besieged his wigged-out tree
all night, green-eyed & rabid.
Into his brain they flashed their teeth.
With hip-flask and deep breathing, he hung in.

A yellow paw reached over
vast savannas, the tall grass purred,
day lay down around him. Eden without tricks.

He stretched. Never had he needed less
nor felt quite so ridiculous. Friends back home
had homes, and incomes, lovers, plans,
were hard at it, not up a baobab –

Alone, unmarked, he stretched & grinned.
His fiends from worse things had protected him.
The problem now was coming down.

Exit

Time to pack it up and move.
This performance is becoming smooth,
Jim notes as he caresses
the one he loves, the 14 strings:

this will become technique.
And he thinks of poor Bill
sentenced to kiss-curl and Rock
Around the Clock for the rest of his natural...

Jings! And those builders in their squash court,
perfect, smooth, without a door,
imprisoned by their mastery...

Hail, and farewells. Outside
the small rain down doth rain
and he must be a journeyman again.

Fictions

This is more arrogance! she shouted and
threw the book at the head it came from.
But this is fiction, he protested, ducking –
You call it fiction, I call it a fucking
liberty. Such a bind to be a man,
all that anger and still can't hit me –

His fist went through the window, dragged
back, hard – She swayed?
He aimed to miss? – sprayed blood and glass.
You need a doctor? *I need*
an editor of genius, what d'ya think?
I think it's just a vein but...

They wait for a taxi in the darkening room.
Fiction? We wrote the book on it?

AT HOME & ABROAD

The Maid & I

'At this stage, I work most closely with the Maid'
New York composer of film scores

It's nothing personal when she slips in
at half-dawn, half-dusk, any drifting
time of day, to make mere solitude complete.
That's how come we get on
so well, so long. You smile, you picture
black seamed stockings, white muslin crown
on hair that's poised to be let down? No,
she is not Naughty Lola –
nor Mrs Mopp! With us it is
importunate to talk or stare;
touch is right out. This fortunate
proximity is all we share.

She has arrived.
You are in the backroom,
by the Steinway, fiddling with the Blues.
You hear her humming as she moves
among the papers and abandoned meals, clearing up
the ashtrays, scripts and coffee cups,
the litter of aloneness. Redeeming fingers touch
your old scores lightly, as if it were yourself
she dusts and settles on the shelf. Praise the maid
who sets out flowers and white clouds
where you might see them and be glad!
The shambles would be total were it not for her.

Now she is singing an old refrain
you can't quite... The sky
is pale, washed clean by rain,
hung up against the evening.
As you attend, a melody floats
through apartment walls so intimately
it is as though you quote yourself –
debris is sorted, order
is invented or restored.
Now she is done. You will work on alone
but that's all right. Grace must have its means.
She flicks the light on as she leaves.

Wallace Stevens in East Fife

If it is anywhere, it must be everywhere –
the mind stumbles after the divine

finding nowhere to halt or grip.
It must be the bush and the wind that wrassles it,

the invisible shook by the visible,
the howl shaken from wind by telephone lines.

It must be speech on the phone
and the silence that resumes

and speech resuming that conversation
between speech and silence which so

shook Sam B., discerning howl in music,
music in the throat of howl.

It must be anytime and at all times,
in the living man and the dead,

in the greatcoat stumbling on the coast,
in the grey coast stumbling through the head.

A North Sea Twist-off

I got oiled on my last night on-shore,
recalling lovers thrown over
shoulders like peel so we could read
the initial of the one we shoulda married
or eaten whole... These drastic shifts
caught up wi me; if I'd worked today
I woulda crushed my hands.

So I've arranged things so I can't,
wrote off fifty grand's machinery.
It has long been my ambition
to make a major blunder;
now I've succeeded, for today at least.
The shaft is plugged, it'll take days more
to extract the cock-up from the core.

*

Too much was going down.
We grouped like para-medics round
a cardiac arrest to bolt
another section to our mile-long probe.
I did it then. Some suspect, nane saw
yon flick of the wrist. We swarmed
in oilskins around catastrophe, pumped down
urgent cooling mud, muttered soothing
angry words, *Come on beauty,
don't break off now*... Too late.
The twist-off was complete.

We shrugged, separated, hurt
by our incompetence, glad of the break.

*

I need the money, I need the work,
I need the green grease on my palms.
These are the first and last,
the fast realities that let us roar
to vanishing-point on our machines.

But there are times I canna watch
the whining, blurry revolutions
screw the planet and ourselves as we
shudder into pay-dirt. Yet I'm convinced
I need the money, so I do.

              *

We can't work till the technicians come.
Could stay on, doing nothing on half-pay,
skimming girlie mags...I'll pass,

chopper out and lie for days somewhere,
a long-abandoned spanner in the grass,
rusting, unadjustable.

She phoned frae Ullapool last night,
thick with the cold, or maybe she
wis greitin, I never will dare ask.

These needs that grow...
It was fun once, now
I've packed my gear – let's go.

Boom-time's over and we aa got shafted.

Bagatelle Dreams
A Canadian rock star has 'a bad case of flu'

TRACK A

My doctor said I have nervous exhaustion.
This must be why I'm water-skiing
on my back along a blue canal.
The wake fans out. I cannot see
what's coming but there is no fear,
all is blue rush and surrender.
Bless the doctors for this ride
of unexamined joy! My nerves are young
in summer; above, the boat's exhaust
makes temporary clouds...

TRACK B

I need a holiday, this must be why
I'm side-stepping the concrete bagatelle
of Yonge Street's high arcade.
Muggers? No fear! I'm wearing
elbow-length gauntlets, my blue
plexi-glass diver's helmet – I
out-weird everyone here. When the steel
ball thunders, I wrap around it,
waving goodbye. I am being rolled
head-first towards more...

FIRST MIX

The doctor said I need a nervous holiday.
This must be why I'm back skiing
high on a street canal, young fans
in my wake. I'm wearing elbow-length muggers
and unexamined joy – doctoring the weird!
All is Blues rush and plexi, a bit mixed.
No fear yet – thunder is a blessing,
the boat steals the gauntlet.
My nerves are rapping, temporarily
exhausting the clouds...

SIDE-TRACK *(second mix)*
Wake, wake. This is your head doctor.
We must be concrete now. No rush,
no fear. Exhausting to step from dreams
into another blessed arcade?
You get so mixed. There are
no muggers, no bagatelles. Waking
is temporary? Balls! You need a summer
holiday from plexi-fans. Blue Gauntlet,
believe me these pills will see you
examining the clouds.

FINAL MIX
Is this concrete, or unexamined dream?
A plexi-question! Exhaust it in surrender.
I can't wear waking, my head skis on
the high canals. Fear is at elbow-length –
will doctor turn mugger, or wave
diverse gauntlets? Thunderous nerves!
The Neil Young fans are singing
'O Steel Summer Clouds'
as they carry me waving
to the Arcadian ball...

In an Italian Field

In the dazzling world the peasants are working.
With bowed heads and backs they drag in line
their dark comb through a field of corn.

They will never get rich. They will never live
in bought houses. Their lives will remain
obscure as their dialect, secret as the women's hair.

Bent as their sickles they shuffle on.
One sings, another mops her brow.
At each row's end they pass the jug around,

at noon chew bread, spit, then sit
for an hour beneath the poplar trees
and silently rise up again...

No wonder we feel flimsy,
returning to our books. The pages blur,
letters start to wave before our eyes –

we are unfocused by the glare outside
where a sickle flashes at the margin of a field,
its shape unchanging as the great stalks yield.

Aide Memoire

Being eighteen,
light-headed, hormonal, daft,
there is much to be said for it.
I said it at length
on the Fife coast that winter.

I donned my Doric cap,
took a stiff whisky,
walked out the door.
In town the lights were blazing
but no one was at home.

What of the white line
I toed by the sea?
The wind blew apart
the clouds round the moon
and I stepped through.

The House-Builder Variations
A workshop – principal materials:
saw, drill, rule, nails, a plain deal table

Unemployed? Growing rusty? You want
a house that is unique – home in on this!
Here's your drill, the hammer-action for concrete,
this is your saw, your rule, your plain deal table.
These are the trees. The compassionate State
awards you with a gross of nails.
Such are your true materials. Confused?
You want to shelve it for today? Believe me,
if you pass on children you must make something
of your own, or live aloner than alone.

A better deal! Unemployed, not unique,
this was his drill: plane it true,
hammer the State, nail it to a tree.
But the old saws were rusty, the rule
was bent, he made nothing at the table.
(He could have said it in spades, but
spades are disallowed materials – you think
association's free?) What frame could house
such passion? It must be concrete, too gross to shelve.
Confused, alone, he passes on today.

Concrete poems? A house of cards, shuffle them
as you will! Deal anyway. What was it she saw
that made the trees seem jungular today?
(Nothing's disallowed, but old drills are bent
as is the State and its materials.)
As a rule, truth's a shelf that takes
unique confusion to nail it to the wall.
Unemployment takes a hammering today
as she sits making passionate children
in her swaying home high in the trees.

Here's what I saw when I took
that hammering: alone is gross.
Let us live in free association,
where is not material. Plain dealing!
Believe me (though I am swaying),
a bent rule is unique. We shall
be shelf-employed! Today is concrete passion.
Nail down this truth:
I love you though the drill be rusty
and the state confused.

Japan
A Romance of Two Empires

'No empire in debt has ever lasted long' – GORE VIDAL

Love fell on you, twice.
The world turned white. You vanished,
you became a shadow on the wall.
The war ended.

You came back from the dead,
speaking our language,
meaning business. This time
you would produce the goods.

> *We met her on time*
> *at the American movie.*
> *We sat through it twice*
> *till we could make it better.*

> *Then we kissed and took her home.*
> *None of us had anything to lose*
> *and after all*
> *we made it cheaper and we made it best.*

> *Now your round eyes flicker when we stir.*
> *You kiss our neck,*
> *we like that. Energetically, we take you again.*
> *You try hard to please. You do. You will.*

For the most part
our protests are conventional
as we subside; arms are weak
when we are in your debt.

And though we sulk,
remembering our time of power,
for the most part
we were tired of Empire.

This is the reconstruction, our royal we
need not be discussed.
You will accept reversal in good time.
Aspire to our eyes and be

a credit. You were tired
and we need each other,
of course we do. This is only
the old order renewed.

It will be a relief
to be so in love,
to be colonised in turn, repent
and loose the burden of our power.

Here in the shadow of our master's kimono
we bite our fingernails and aspire.

Homage to Master Berryman

Sunk sloop John B., I have to talk at you,
seeing you around no more. (Slid off
the bridge, waved not.) Give me your due
deaf ear & pardon, who hassled audience with Yeats
before you was halfways great.
Them dislocations still appeal – appalling

high-minded & randy, compulsive chaser,
awful and true. Suffered for it too –
booming out & cringing in,
rampant & trembling for thirty years. Resigned
great shade, those ways are out:
we dream of reputation, and we fall in line.

Well-mannered, discreet, soberly
polishing the obvious – *Are these folks for real?*
you enquire. *Who live by the word must be
ready to die by it. Else not serious people.*
I don't want be badly & cracked! *But that's the deal,*
But...for this Dream Song form, John, I need more lines –

Thanks. Art, decency, sanity – can't square it?
Loopy Cal, Mr Lowell *to you, scampered under
my tree all afternoon, throwing up sticks. We laughed,
were briefly happy & unmarked. Were not all so bad.* There were others
honed for the chop? *One
claimed dying was an art,*

did it so badly she finally succeeded. And succeeded.
And your fearful double Henry, sunk with his gripes
& lust & glass? *Yet raged & wept
at McCarthy, the dying children in Delhi.
And deluded Delmore,   Anne who tolled too early –*
All you crazy bad and great: *wus Serious People, pal.*

Were you still with us I could not breathe,
you being too much. Brow-beater –
tearful, fearful, loyal & all – I take my leave.
My times you urge and warn and flash
dark lightning exact. I commit you & salute
one friend of timing   wayward, absolute.

Mexico

'Doña Barbara, que devora a los hombres'

In the truck she let the Octopus
open her shirt, also the blonde
divorcee's – it was her dive
through dark heat, she could not rise
till everything was lifted from her.
She had kept herself apart for years,
virtuous, no affairs with lecturers
as she surveyed the glittering
surface and swell of Yanqui power.
Night rose round her and she laughed,
appalled, assenting as he gripped
the blonde heads back, rinsed mouths
with beer and marijuana. Out the window
her hand spread, released wallet and I.D.
What a burden righteousness becomes!
The divorcee peeled mangoes with her nails,
licked dark fingers one by one before
inserting them beneath her skirt.

Cooler up front with the driver
who drank white rum and kissed her eyes
while he spoke poetry about the moon
flowering over Vera Cruz, the shack
where she could stay, indebted, in roses,
good and chattel like his country
to the Yanqui dollar. Headlights
skewered the jungle, her eyes streamed.
He spoke beautifully but was gentle-souled,
was not the Octopus who devoured *gringa*.
She buttoned her shirt and clambered back.
The divorcee lay unconscious on the sacks,
graceless, released. What had passed here?
The Octopus shrugged. Self-respect
had kept her on the surface all these years,
buoyed up by her critique – time
to meet what lay beneath.

There was sand, water, men in a circle,
some ceremony she could not master
nor deconstruct away. One shot
white arrows at the moon and fell
twitching, ecstatic. The Octopus took peyote,
his tongues thrust mush into her mouth;
she nodded, choked, tore off her shirt
and spun the world round her jittery hips
as though it were a hula-hoop and she
a child in her Mid-West backyard.
None looked her way, he swam,
she could still run for it.

He found her dreaming on the sand,
arrow in her fist. Crossing himself,
Doña Barbara, he took her to the truck.
Conscious and unconscious breasts compared
were found wanting. Leeched upon,
she strained to drain into his mouth;
her inverted nipple hurt, swelled,
would not come free. Another town,
she stumbled out for beer and tacos –
no shirt, no money, still she knew
blonde hair, white skin would see her through,
and despaired. How may power resign
from its high place? This nervy diver
had come teetering to the edge…

At the end there was a room. Men sleeping
stirred in their hammocks when she plunged
to meet the Octopus in the tightening net.
They grappled, clasped, fought limb to limb,
snapped beak to beak till in the mesh
he suckered the Barbarian. She clasped the arrow,
he rose shouting – puddled, ecstatic,
she drifted while he lay harpooned.

Then there were many hands, some kind.

They carried her out at dawn,
trembling, bloody, white as salt.
A bus pulled up, she gripped her blanket
then rose and in the loving tongue
she mastered her first lie.

　　　*

Her thumb on the inside of my arm
still lightly stroked the vein.
We lay in her hammock strung above
the porch, Toronto, Little Italy;
the old insomniac next door
pruned tomatoes in the dark and hummed
his exile, it would soon be day.
*'But that was in another country
and besides, the hombre's dead.'*
I held her, sweating, knowing she'd said
all that she would say.

A Good Talking To

When the din fades
and ghosts of the day disperse
into the wallpaper of an ordinary room
a voice speaks quietly
and I listen.

It has recently begun
to address the divine.
Do not be alarmed!
I am always polite
it says in an aside.

What does it say to the divine
this pertinent voice?
please   sustain me   thank you
Communications are simple
among the adept.

I would wish to be someone
who could address without blushing
a vast stadium
even if the multitudes
have picked up their coats and streamed home.